The Worship PIANO METHOD LEVEL 1

By Wendy Stevens and Teresa Ledford

T0079440

PLAYBACK+
Speed • Pitch • Balance • Loop

To access audio visit:
www.halleonard.com/mylibrary

Enter Code
4051-1228-3110-2064

ISBN 978-1-61774-040-4

HAL•LEONARD®

Scripture taken from the NEW AMERICAN STANDARD BIBLE®,
Copyright © 1960,1962,1963,1968,1971,1972,1973,
1975,1977,1995 by The Lockman Foundation.
Used by permission.

Scripture taken from the New Century Version.
Copyright © 2005 by Thomas Nelson, Inc.
Used by permission. All rights reserved.

Visit Hal Leonard Online at
www.halleonard.com

Contact Us:
Hal Leonard
7777 West Bluemound Road
Milwaukee, WI 53213
Email: info@halleonard.com

In Europe contact:
Hal Leonard Europe Limited
Distribution Centre, Newmarket Road
Bury St Edmunds, Suffolk, IP33 3YB
Email: info@halleonardeurope.com

In Australia contact:
Hal Leonard Australia Pty. Ltd.
4 Lentara Court
Cheltenham, Victoria, 3192 Australia
Email: info@halleonard.com.au

READING MUSIC – A Basic Overview

Here are some music facts you will need to know as you begin this book. If you're already familiar with these, congratulations! You're off to a great start. If everything is new to you, don't worry. Some of this information will be reviewed as you go along.

NOTES AND RESTS

Notes represent sound, while **rests** represent silence.

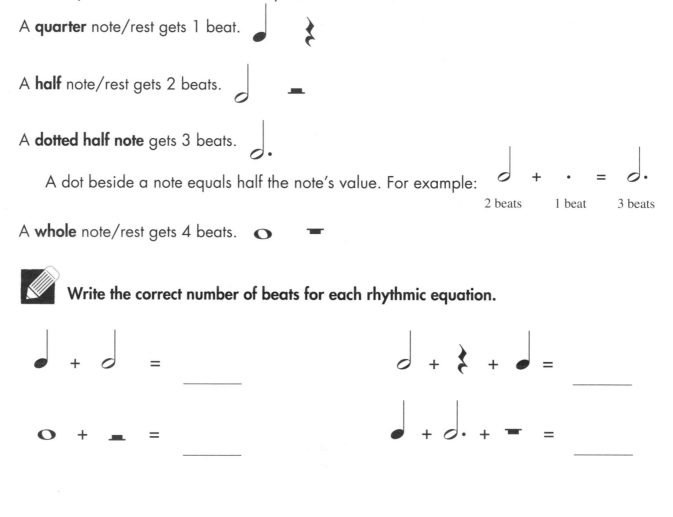

A **quarter** note/rest gets 1 beat.

A **half** note/rest gets 2 beats.

A **dotted half note** gets 3 beats.

A dot beside a note equals half the note's value. For example:

2 beats   1 beat   3 beats

A **whole** note/rest gets 4 beats.

Write the correct number of beats for each rhythmic equation.

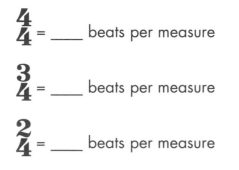

TIME SIGNATURE

The **top number** of the time signature tells you how many beats are in each measure.

measure

4/4 = _____ beats per measure

3/4 = _____ beats per measure

2/4 = _____ beats per measure

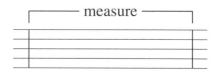

The **bottom number** tells you which kind of note gets 1 beat. In the given examples, the "4" on the bottom means the quarter note gets 1 beat.

$$\frac{4}{4} = \frac{4}{\text{♩}}$$

RHYTHM

Clap the following rhythms. Count each beat out loud.

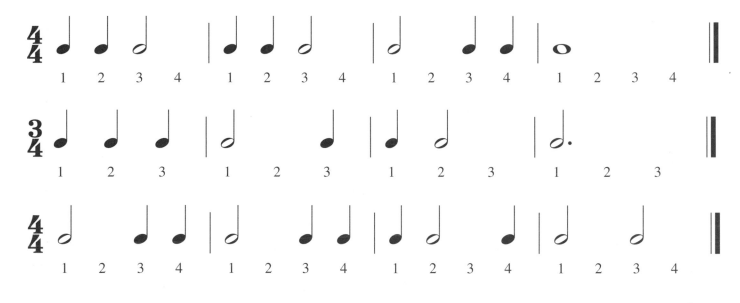

WHITE KEY NOTE NAMES

These are the names of the white keys:

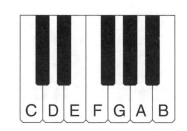

Write the correct letter name under each starred key to complete this Bible verse.

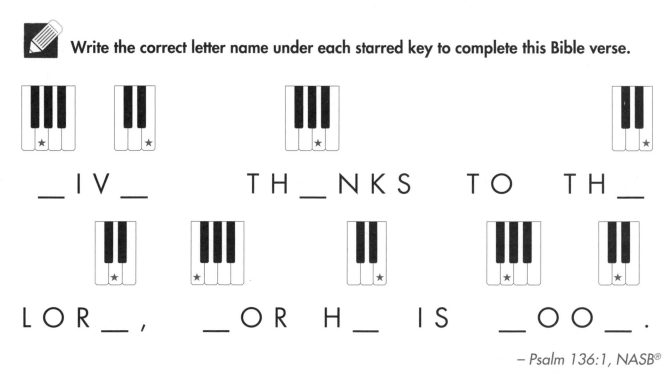

_IV_   TH_NKS   TO   TH_

LOR_,   _OR H_ IS   _OO_.

– Psalm 136:1, NASB®

THE STAFF

The staff has five lines and four spaces.

Notes can sit on a line or in a space.

on a line   in a space

Notes in the **treble clef** are usually played with the right hand.

R.H.

Notes in the **bass clef** are usually played with the left hand.

L.H.

Middle C may be played with either hand, depending on the clef.

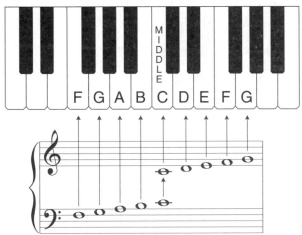

L.H.

R.H.

STAFF NOTE NAMES

MIDDLE

F G A B C D E F G

Here's a handy reference for note names. You will learn all of these notes and more in this book.

MUSICAL SYMBOLS

A **repeat sign** tells you to return to the beginning, or back to a reverse-facing repeat sign.

A **final bar line** means you have reached the end of a piece.

Dynamics tell you how loud or soft you should play.

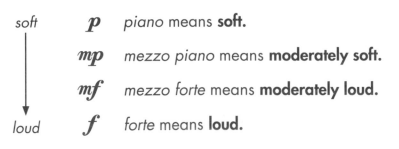

soft

p   piano means **soft.**

mp   mezzo piano means **moderately soft.**

mf   mezzo forte means **moderately loud.**

loud

f   forte means **loud.**

POSTURE AT THE PIANO

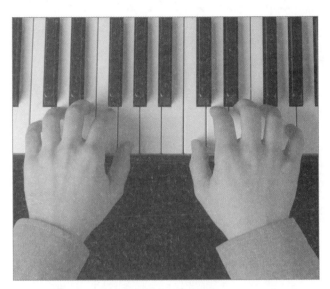

When sitting at the piano, keep your back straight, your shoulders relaxed, and your forearms level with the keyboard.

Your fingers should be slightly curved as you play. Your thumb will play on its side.

FINGER NUMBERS

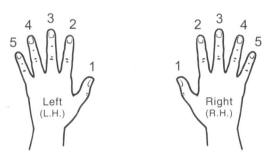

Left (L.H.)

Right (R.H.)

 Write L.H. or R.H. on the inside of each hand. Then write the finger number above each finger wearing a ring.

Example: **3**

R.H.

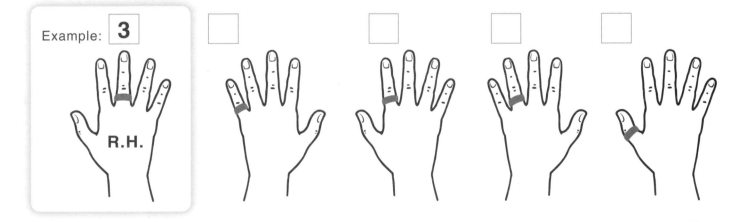

"Whatever your hand finds to do, do it with all your might."
– Ecclesiastes 9:10, NASB

Now you're ready to play your first piece!

Treble Clef: Middle C, Treble G

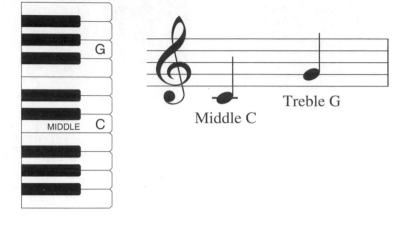

"…His name will be called Wonderful Counselor, Mighty God, Eternal Father, Prince of Peace."
– Isaiah 9:6, NASB

TRACKS 1-2

Holy Is Your Name

By Wendy Stevens

Cheerfully ♩ = 120

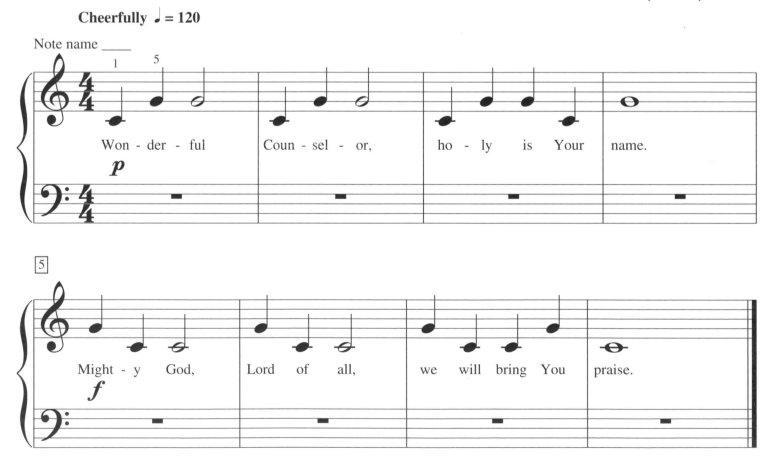

Note name _____

Won - der - ful Coun - sel - or, ho - ly is Your name.

p

Might - y God, Lord of all, we will bring You praise.

f

Bass Clef: Middle C, Bass F

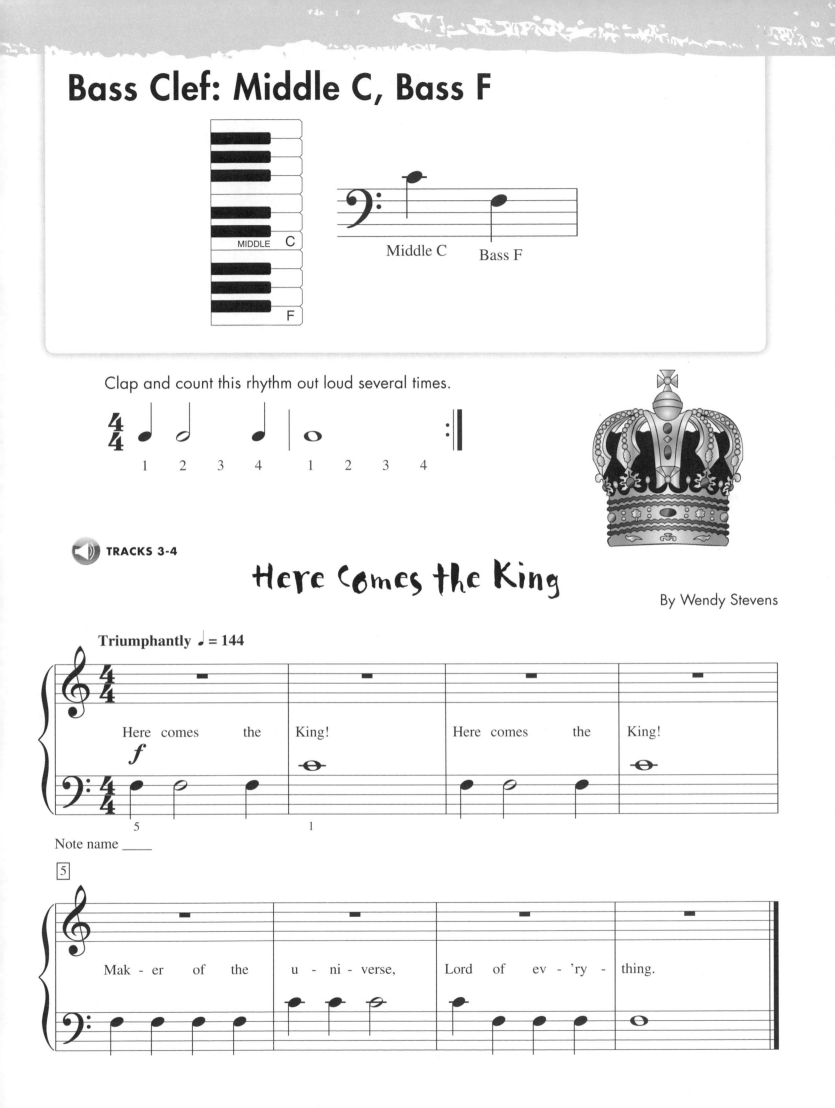

Clap and count this rhythm out loud several times.

TRACKS 3-4

Here Comes the King

By Wendy Stevens

Triumphantly ♩ = 144

Here comes the King! Here comes the King!

f

5   1

Note name ____

5

Mak - er of the u - ni - verse, Lord of ev - 'ry - thing.

Steps in the Treble Clef

Notes moving from a line to the next space or a space to the next line are called **steps**.

G F E D C

new notes

TRACKS 5-6

Your Love Will Endure

Smoothly ♩ = 116

By Teresa Ledford

Note name ____

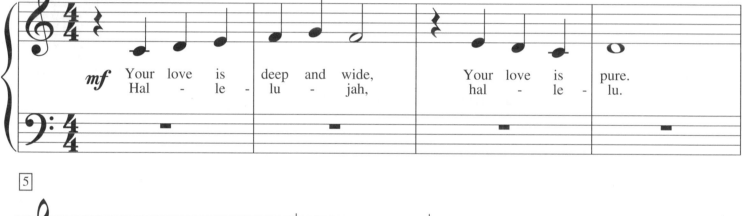

mf Your love is deep and wide, Your love is pure.
Hal - le - lu - jah, hal - le - lu.

You're al - ways faith - ful and Your love ___ will en - dure.
Hal - le - lu - jah, Your love ___ will en - dure.

Accompaniment (Student plays one octave higher than written.)

Smoothly ♩ = 116

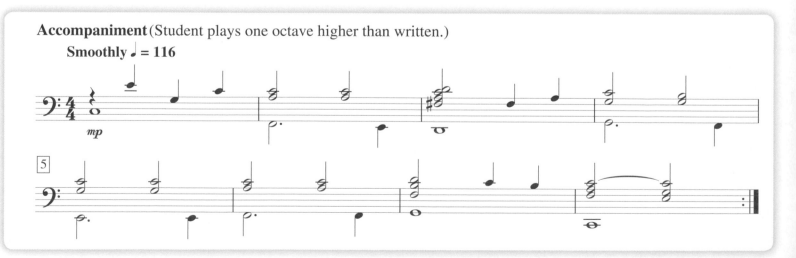

mp

8

Steps in the Bass Clef

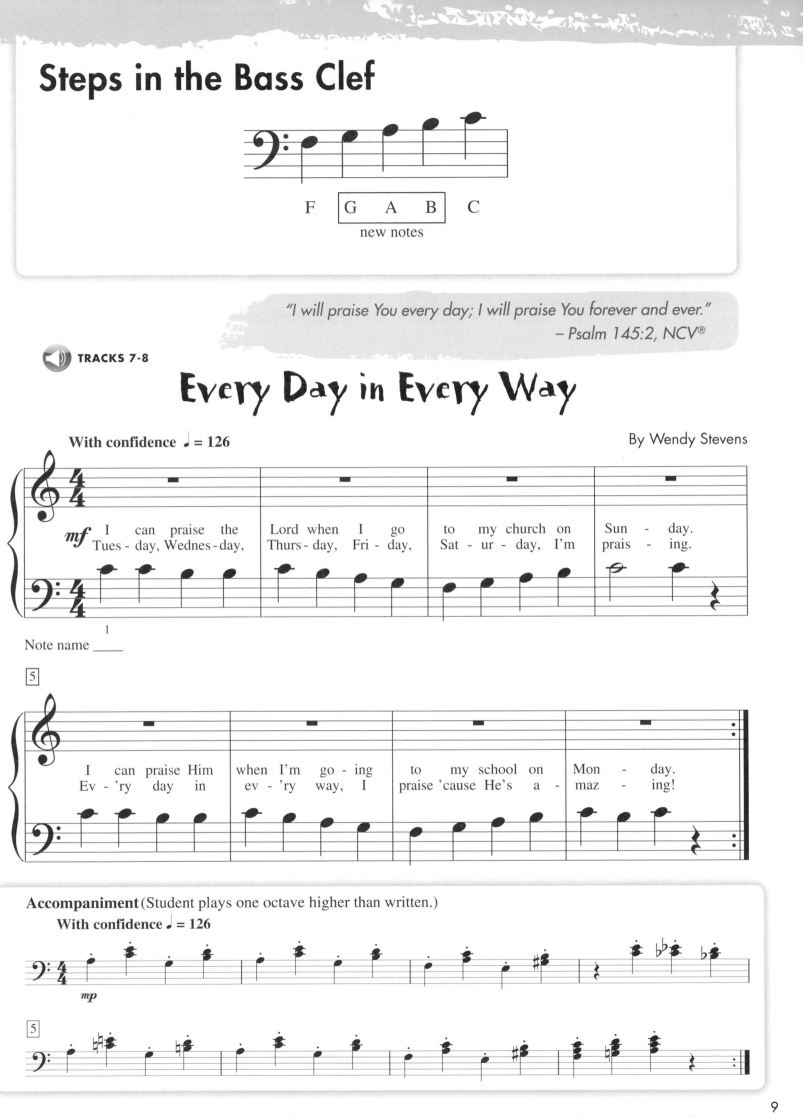

F **G A B** C

new notes

TRACKS 7-8

Every Day in Every Way

With confidence ♩ = 126

By Wendy Stevens

mf I can praise the Lord when I go to my church on Sun - day.
Tues - day, Wednes - day, Thurs - day, Fri - day, Sat - ur - day, I'm prais - ing.

Note name _____

I can praise Him when I'm go - ing to my school on Mon - day.
Ev - 'ry day in ev - 'ry way, I praise 'cause He's a - maz - ing!

Accompaniment (Student plays one octave higher than written.)

With confidence ♩ = 126

mp

9

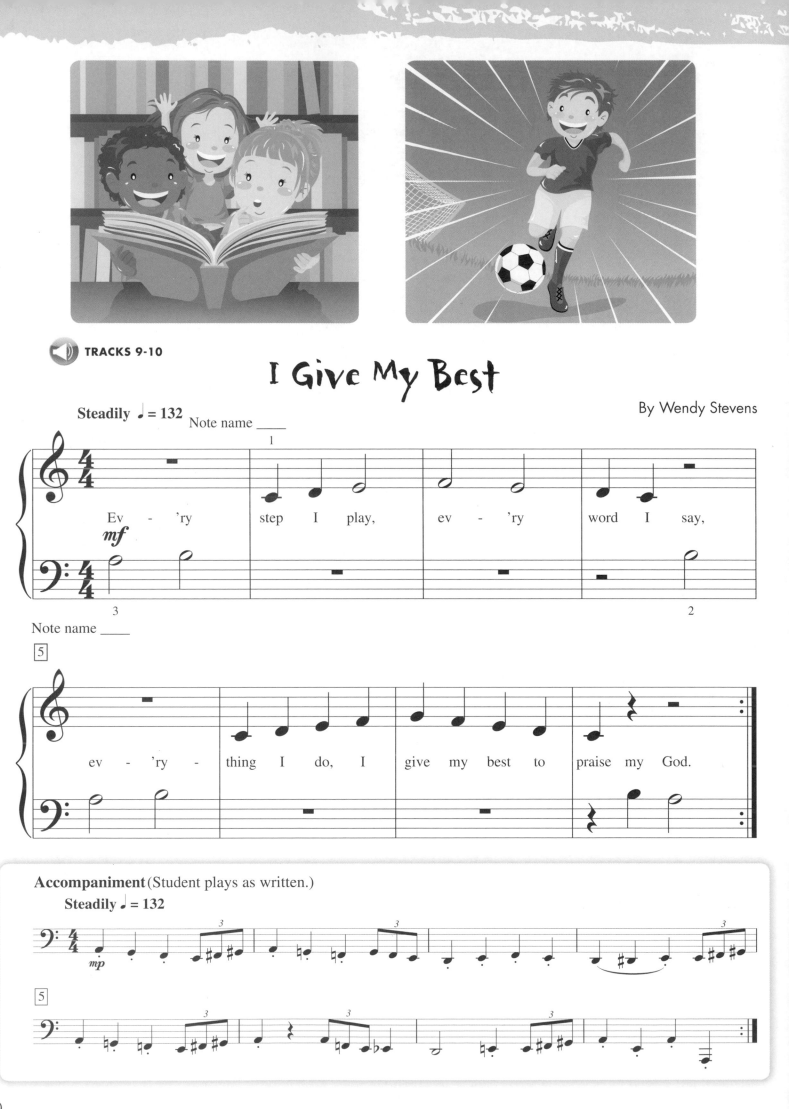

TRACKS 9-10

I Give My Best

By Wendy Stevens

Steadily ♩ = 132 Note name ____

Ev - 'ry step I play, ev - 'ry word I say,

mf

3

Note name ____

5

ev - 'ry - thing I do, I give my best to praise my God.

Accompaniment (Student plays as written.)

Steadily ♩ = 132

mp

5

TRACKS 11-12

Where Is God?

By Wendy Stevens

Thoughtfully ♩ = 108

Note name ____

Where is God when I am scared? Is He with me in the night?

Note name ____

"I am here," He says to me, "till the morn - ing light."

Accompaniment (Student plays two octaves higher than written.)

Thoughtfully ♩ = 108

With pedal

Ties

A tie connects two notes on the same line or space.

Hold the note for the combined value of both notes.

How many beats is
this note held? _____

🔊 **TRACKS 13-14**

I've Got Peace Like a River

Traditional
Arranged by Wendy Stevens

Peacefully ♩ = 120

Note name ____

I've got peace like a riv - er, I've got peace like a

mp

Note name ____

Accompaniment (Student plays one octave higher than written.)

Peacefully ♩ = 120

p

My Song of Praise (C D E)

 Compose your own praise song using only C D E. Write your note names in the boxes, and play them with the rhythm given. Use both steps and repeated notes.

God is great and God is good; let us thank Him for our food.

By His hands we all are fed; thank You, Lord, for dai - ly bread.

Composing Tip: Try using the same notes in measures 1 and 5. This will make your song easier to sing and remember.

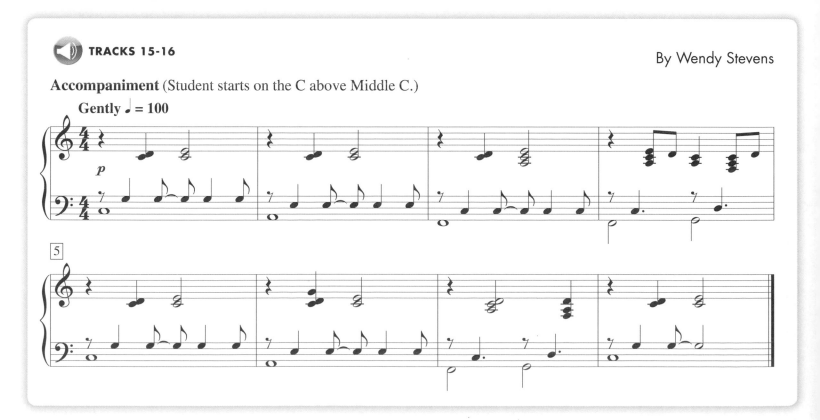

TRACKS 15-16

By Wendy Stevens

Accompaniment (Student starts on the C above Middle C.)

Gently ♩ = 100

Note Name Review

 Match each letter name with the correct note on the keyboard and staff, as shown below.

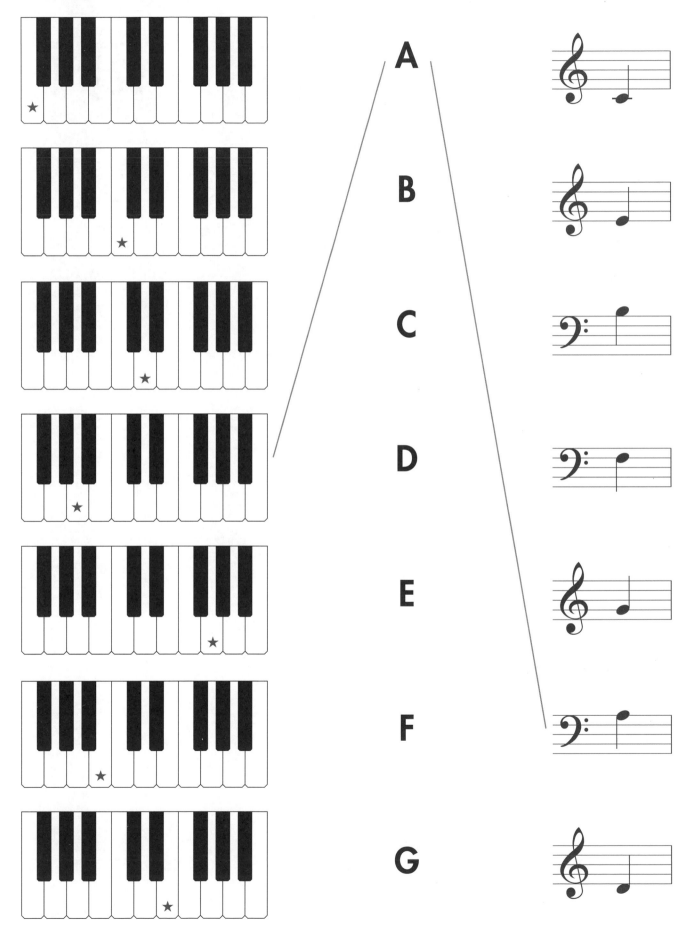

Skips

On the staff: A skip moves from a line to a line or a space to a space.

On the keyboard: Your fingers will skip one white key.

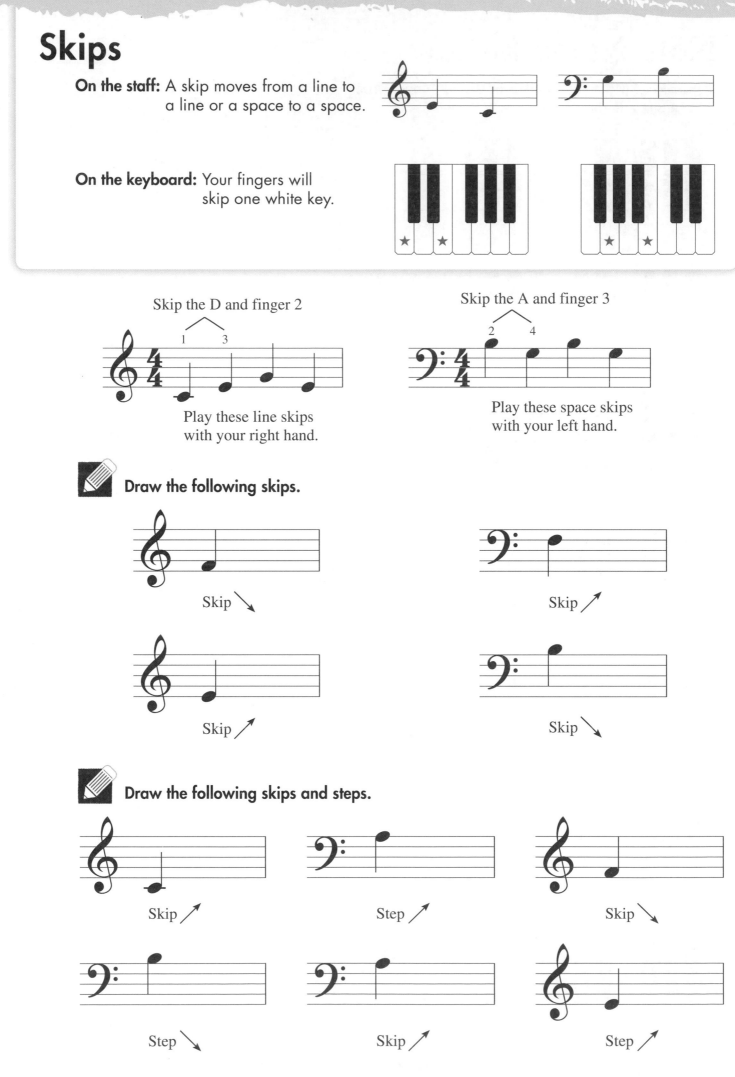

Skip the D and finger 2

Play these line skips with your right hand.

Skip the A and finger 3

Play these space skips with your left hand.

Draw the following skips.

Skip ↘

Skip ↗

Skip ↗

Skip ↘

Draw the following skips and steps.

Skip ↗

Step ↗

Skip ↘

Step ↘

Skip ↗

Step ↗

"The Lord says, 'I will make you wise and show you where to go.
I will guide you and watch over you.'"
– Psalm 32:8, NCV

Always Watching

 **TRACKS 17-18**

By Wendy Stevens

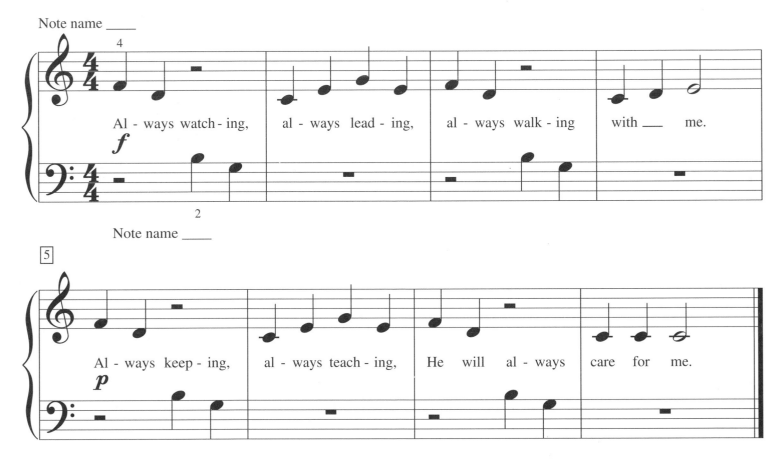

Note name ____

With confidence ♩ = 126

Al - ways watch - ing, al - ways lead - ing, al - ways walk - ing with ___ me.

f

Note name ____

Al - ways keep - ing, al - ways teach - ing, He will al - ways care for me.

p

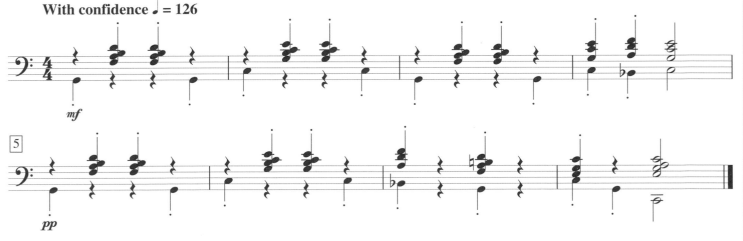

Accompaniment (Student plays one octave higher than written.)

With confidence ♩ = 126

mf

pp

My God Is So Great, So Strong and So Mighty

TRACKS 19-20

Find and circle the four skips in this piece.

Traditional
Arranged by Wendy Stevens

Happily ♩ = 152

Note name ____

My God is so great, so strong and so might - y; there's noth - ing my God can - not do! The moun - tains are His, the riv - ers are

Accompaniment (Student plays one octave higher than written.)

Happily ♩ = 152

His, the stars are His hand - i - work, too.

My God is so great, so strong and so

might - y; there's noth - ing my God can - not do! _____

Pickup Notes

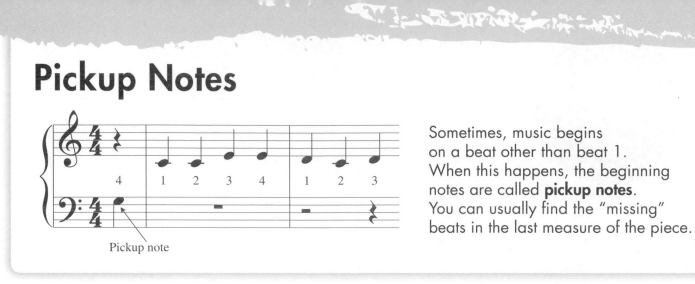

Pickup note

Sometimes, music begins on a beat other than beat 1. When this happens, the beginning notes are called **pickup notes**. You can usually find the "missing" beats in the last measure of the piece.

Praise God, From Whom All Blessings Flow

 Find and circle all the skips in this piece. (One is hidden between the hands.)

TRACKS 21-22

Words by Thomas Ken
Music Attributed to Louis Bourgeois
Arranged by Wendy Stevens

With reverence ♩ = 108

Note name ____

Note name ____

Praise God, from whom all bless - ings flow. ____

____ Praise Him, all crea - tures here be - low. Praise

Accompaniment (Student plays one octave higher than written.)

With reverence ♩ = 108

20

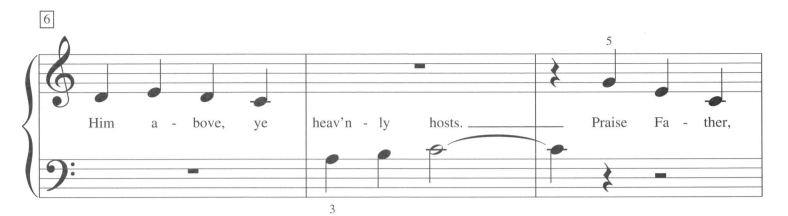

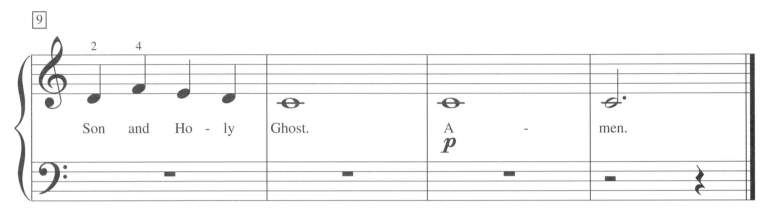

 Name 5 good gifts you have been given by God.

_____   _____

_____   _____

_____

WRITING LYRICS

Sometimes, new words are composed for old hymn tunes. You can practice being a lyricist (composer of song words) and write another verse to this hymn. Use some of the good gifts you listed above to fill in the blanks.

Praise God for all my _____ and _____. (one-syllable words)

Praise Him for all my _____ and _____. (one-syllable words)

Praise Him because He _____ _____ _____. (one-syllable words)

Praise Father, Son and Holy Ghost. Amen.

Name That Hymn!

Title: _____

Find and circle all the skips in this piece. (Some are hidden between the hands.)
Do you know the title of this hymn? If so, write it in the blank above.

TRACKS 23-24

Words by Anna B. Warner
Music by William B. Bradbury
Arranged by Wendy Stevens

Gently ♩ = 120

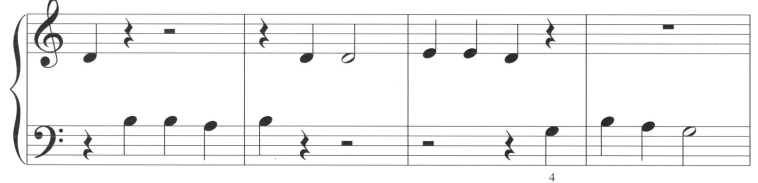

Accompaniment (Student plays one octave higher than written.)

Gently ♩ = 120

Step and Skip Review

 FIND THE HIDDEN SYMBOL!

1. Write "ST" under each step, and "SK" under each skip.
2. Color the ST boxes blue and the SK boxes brown to reveal the hidden symbol.

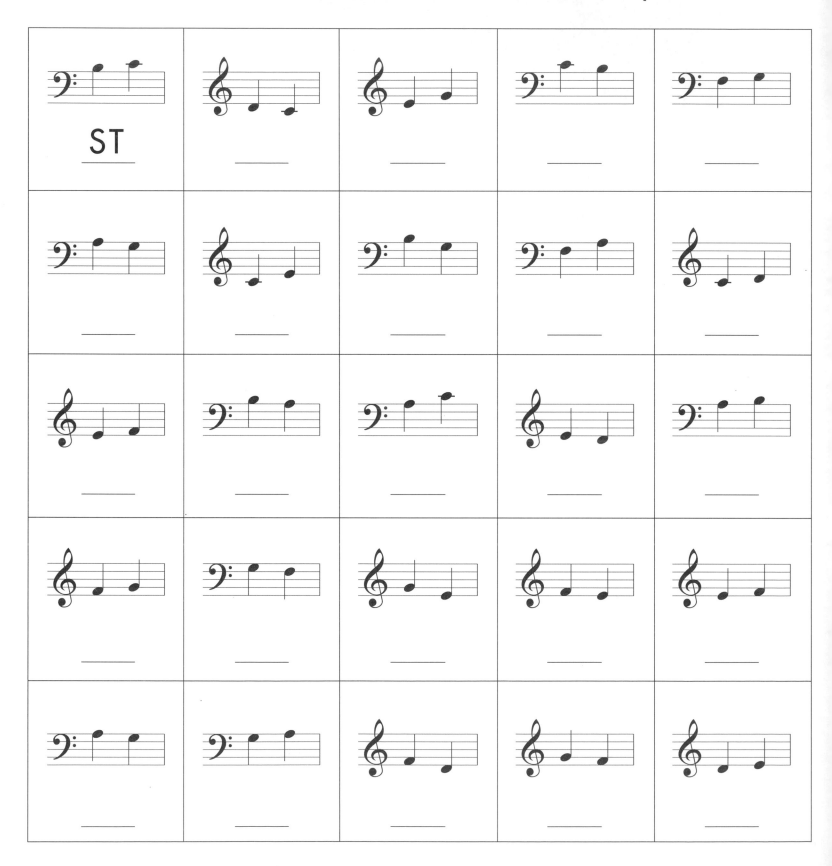

My Melody of Praise (C D E F G)

IMPROVISING A MELODY

When playing for a worship service, pianists sometimes need to **improvise** (make up a tune as they play).

 Practice improvising your own melody using C D E F G.
Use steps, skips, and repeated notes.

Improvising Tip: Try to use a combination of long and short notes as you improvise.

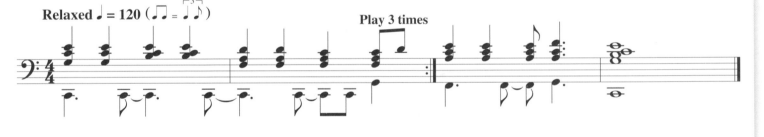

TRACKS 25-26

By Wendy Stevens

Accompaniment (Student plays one octave higher than written.)

New Note: Treble A

 TRACKS 27-28

Thanksgiving Prayer

Find and circle the Treble A in this piece.

Words adapted from Ralph Waldo Emerson's poem
Music by Wendy Stevens

Prayerfully ♩ = 108

Note name ____

For each new morn - ing with its light, for

Note name ____

Accompaniment (Student plays two octaves higher than written.)

Prayerfully ♩ = 108

With pedal

rest and shel - ter of the night; health and food,
mf

love and friends, for all things Thy good - ness sends.
mp

mp

p

Come, Thou Almighty King

Traditional
Music by Felice de Giardini
Arranged by Wendy Stevens

come and reign o - ver us, An - cient of Days!
(cross L.H. over R.H.)

Introductions

When people sing together, it is helpful for the pianist to play an introduction (or "intro") so that everyone knows when to begin.

You can often play the last four measures of a hymn as an intro.

Gather a group of people around the piano to sing "Come, Thou Almighty King." Play the last four measures as the intro.

New Note: Treble B

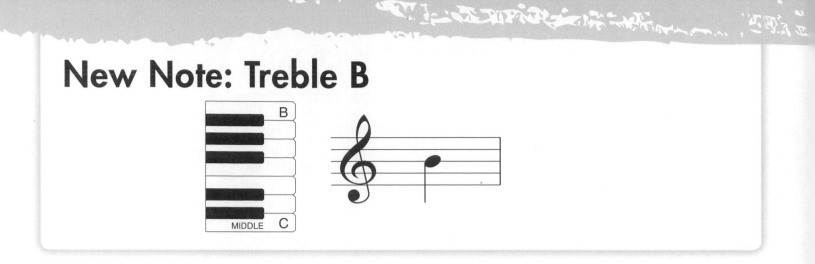

Sometimes, God wants us to worship Him by being still and just listening to what He says.

Damper Pedal

 **TRACKS 31-32**

Quiet Waters

By Wendy Stevens

Reflectively ♩ = 108 *Hold damper pedal down throughout piece.*

Note name ____

Note name ____

5

*"…The whole crowd of disciples began to praise God
joyfully with a loud voice for all the miracles which they had seen…
Some of the Pharisees in the crowd said to Him, 'Teacher, rebuke Your disciples.'*

But Jesus answered, 'I tell you, if these become silent, the stones will cry out!'"
– Luke 19:37-40, NASB

TRACKS 33-34

Sing and Shout!

By Wendy Stevens

Note name ____

If we don't sing and shout, if we don't sing and wor-ship,

Note name ____

if we don't praise Him, then the rocks will cry out! ____

Accompaniment (Student plays one octave higher than written.)

With a groove ♩ = 144

31

New Notes: Bass C, D, E

TRACKS 35-36

All Day My Heart Is Singing

Joyfully ♩ = 138

By Wendy Stevens

Note name ____

All day my heart is sing-ing, morn - ing and af - ter - noon.

Note name ____

Night comes and still I'm sing-ing, "Al - le - lu - ia, Al - le - lu,

Accompaniment (Student plays two octaves higher than written.)

Joyfully ♩ = 138

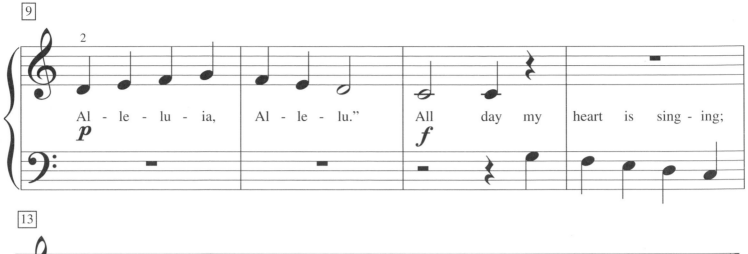

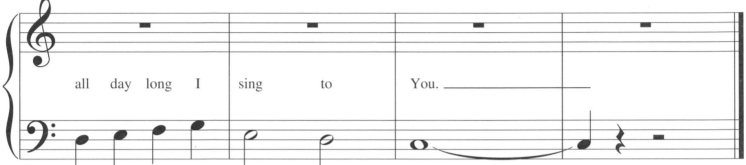

"I am always praising You; all day long I honor You.
— Psalm 71:8, NCV

Note Review

Write the names of these notes in the blanks.

Play these notes with your R.H. 2nd finger, and then your L.H. 2nd finger on the repeat. Hold the damper pedal down throughout the exercise.

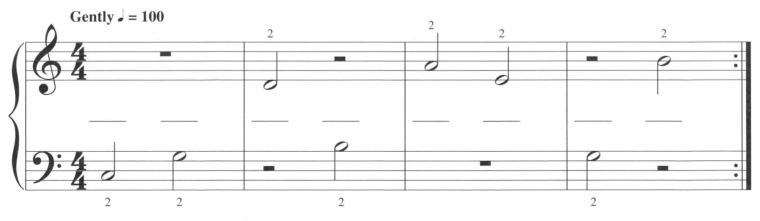

Joyful, Joyful, We Adore Thee

Words by Henry van Dyke
Music by Ludwig van Beethoven
Melody from *Ninth Symphony*
Arranged by Teresa Ledford

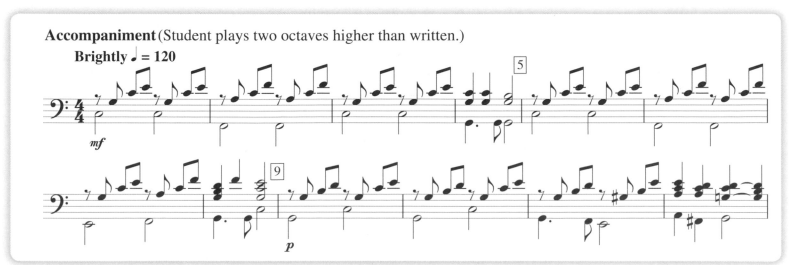

When the last part of a song is repeated or stretched out, it is called a **tag**.

Tags

Musicians create tags by repeating and/or stretching out the last part of a song. (see measures 17–20 of "Joyful, Joyful, We Adore Thee.")

 Play the last line from "Come, Thou Almighty King" below, and then experiment with ways to add a tag. Here are some suggestions: Move up to a higher C, gradually slow the tag down, or make each note longer in measure 15.

Now, go back to page 28 and play the entire hymn, adding your tag.

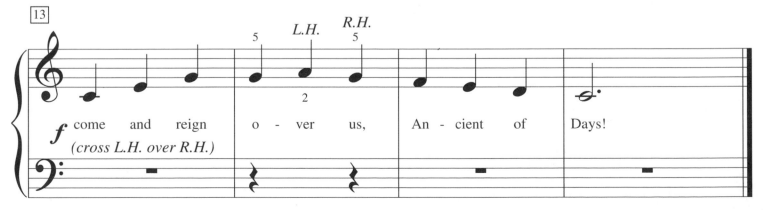

Oh, How I Love Jesus

Happily ♩ = 152

Words by Frederick Whitfield
Traditional American Melody
Arranged by Teresa Ledford

Note name ____

Note name ____

Accompaniment (Student plays two octaves higher than written.)

Happily ♩ = 152

Intervals: 2nds, 3rds

Melodic 2nd

Harmonic 2nd

A 2nd is the same as a step.

A 2nd is found on a line and the next space, or a space and the next line.

Melodic 2nds are played separately. Harmonic 2nds are played together.

A 3rd is the same as a skip.

A 3rd is found on a line and the next line, or a space and the next space.

Melodic 3rds are played separately. Harmonic 3rds are played together.

Melodic 3rd

Harmonic 3rd

 **Circle the harmonic 3rds below. Draw a box around the harmonic 2nds.**

Fill the Air with Praise

 **TRACKS 41-42**

By Wendy Stevens

Happily ♩ = 152

Note name ____
1

f

Sing this tune with me,   sing it   hap - pi - ly.

mp (Play the L.H. notes softer than the R.H. melody.)

Note ____ 1
names ____ 3

Note ____
names ____

5

Sing   it   loud and clear, and   fill   the   air   with   praise.

Staccato & Legato

Staccato marks are small dots on the tops or bottoms of notes. They tell you to play the notes in a short and separated way.

A **slur** is a curved line connecting different notes. It tells you that the notes are to be played *legato*, which means smooth and connected. Most of the time, worship songs are sung in a *legato* style, so slurs are not always necessary.

 **Repeat this excercise until you feel confident with the left-hand movement.**

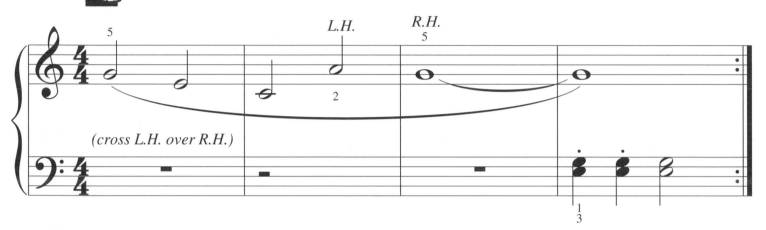

(cross L.H. over R.H.)

🔊 **TRACKS 43-44**

What a Mighty God We Serve

Traditional
Arranged by Teresa Ledford

Brightly ♩ = 160

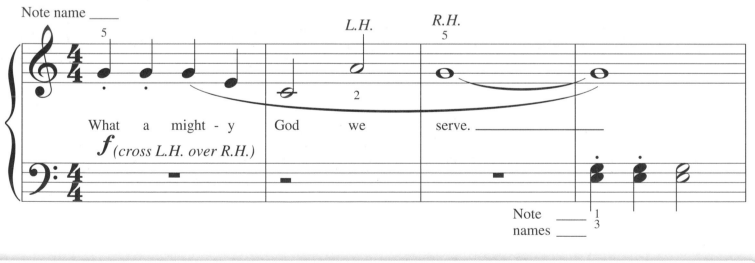

Note name ____

What a might-y God we serve. _____

f (cross L.H. over R.H.)

Note names ____ ____

Accompaniment (Student plays one octave higher than written.)

Brightly ♩ = 160

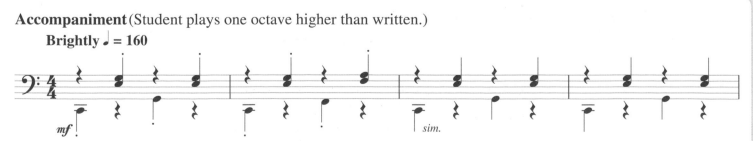

mf   *sim.*

5

What a might-y God we serve. _____

9

L.H. *R.H.* *L.H.* *R.H.*

An - gels bow be - fore ___ Him, heav'n and earth a - dore ___ Him.

13

What a might-y God we serve. _____

5

9

13

My Melody of Praise (D E F G A)

Praise bands will often **vamp** (repeat a pattern) before they play a song, or between verses of a song. This gives the worship leader time to introduce the song, pray, or just let people worship silently.

1. Play the pattern of 2nds and 3rds below while your teacher plays the accompaniment.
2. Vamp the pattern until you are ready to begin improvising your melody. (The CD will repeat the pattern once.)
3. Improvise your melody. Your teacher will follow your lead.

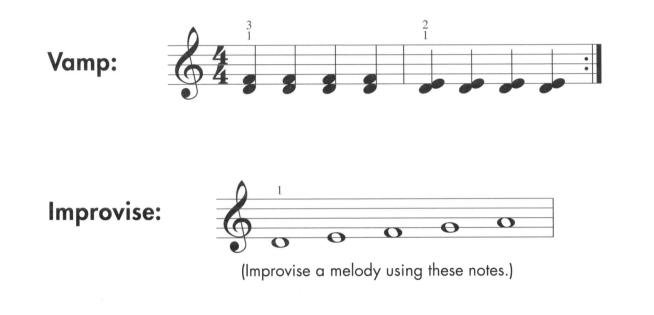

Vamp:

Improvise:

(Improvise a melody using these notes.)

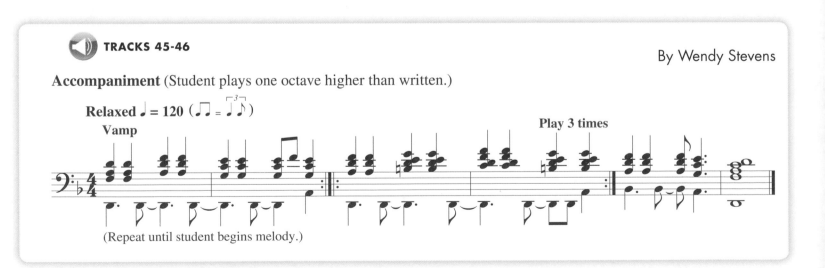

TRACKS 45-46

By Wendy Stevens

Accompaniment (Student plays one octave higher than written.)

Relaxed ♩ = 120

Vamp

Play 3 times

(Repeat until student begins melody.)

Intervals: 4ths

A 4th is found on a line and a space, or a space and a line.
It skips two white keys on the keyboard.

Melodic 4th   Harmonic 4th

 **Circle the 4ths in these examples.**

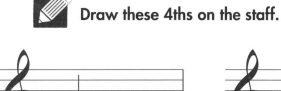

 **Draw these 4ths on the staff.**

4th ↗   4th ↘

4th ↘   4th ↗

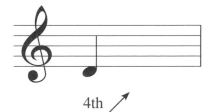 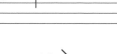

4th ↗   4th ↘

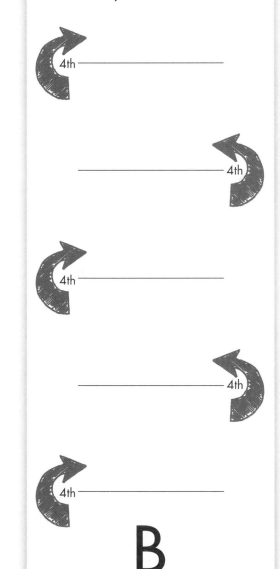

1. Starting at the bottom, write the name of the note that would be a 4th above each note.

2. Play the notes from bottom to top while holding down the damper pedal. Start with any B below middle C.

4th _____

_____ 4th

4th _____

_____ 4th

4th _____

B

For the Beauty of the Earth

Find and circle the two 4ths in this piece.

Words by Folliot S. Pierpoint
Music by Conrad Kocher
Arranged by Teresa Ledford

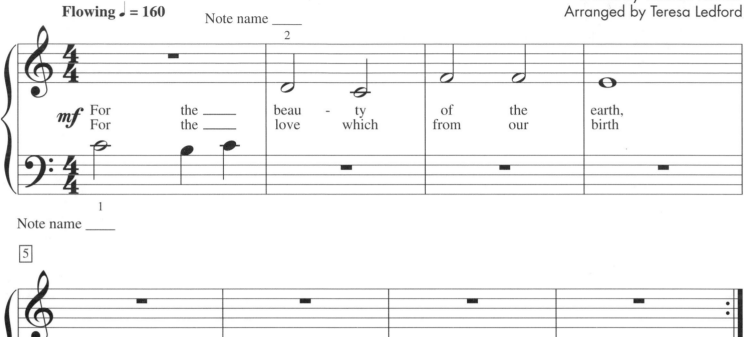

Note name ____

Flowing ♩ = 160

Note name ____

For the _____ beau - ty of the earth,
For the _____ love which from our birth

for the glo - ry of the skies.
o - ver and a - round us lies:

Accompaniment (Student plays one octave higher than written.)

Flowing ♩ = 160

9

Lord of all, to Thee we raise

f

13

this, our hymn of grate - ful praise.

Hear the Bells

Joyfully ♩ = 176 *Hold damper pedal down throughout piece.*

By Teresa Ledford

Intervals: 5ths

A 5th is found on a line and a line, or a space and a space.
It skips three white keys on the keyboard.

Melodic 5th   Harmonic 5th

 Circle the 5ths in these examples.

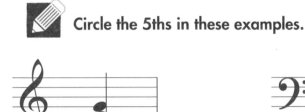

 1. Draw the following 5ths on the staff, using half notes.

2. Play this line of music, holding down the damper pedal.

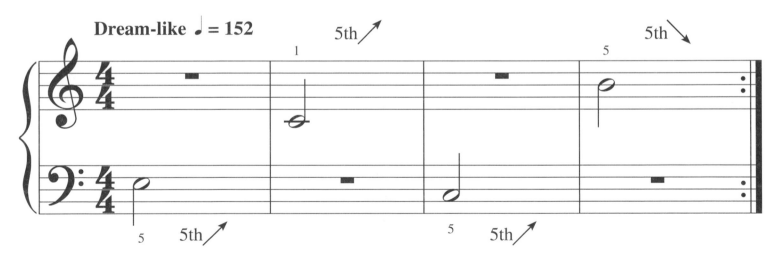

 Write the answer to the following interval riddles:

1. Start on G. Go up a 5th. Go down a 3rd. Go up a 2nd. What note is this? _____

2. Start on D. Go down a 4th. Go up a 3rd. Go down a 5th. What note is this? _____

3. Start on F. Go up a 3rd. Go down a 2nd. Go down a 4th. What note is this? _____

 **Find and circle the three 5ths in this piece. (Two are hidden between the hands.)**

Praise to the Lord, the Almighty

Words by Joachim Neander
Translated by Catherine Winkworth
Music from *Erneuerten Gesangbuch*
Arranged by Teresa Ledford

 Gather a group of people around the piano to sing "Praise to the Lord, the Almighty." Play an intro (the last four measures) and sing this majestic hymn together.

46

Ritardando

Ritardando (or *rit.*) means to gradually slow down.

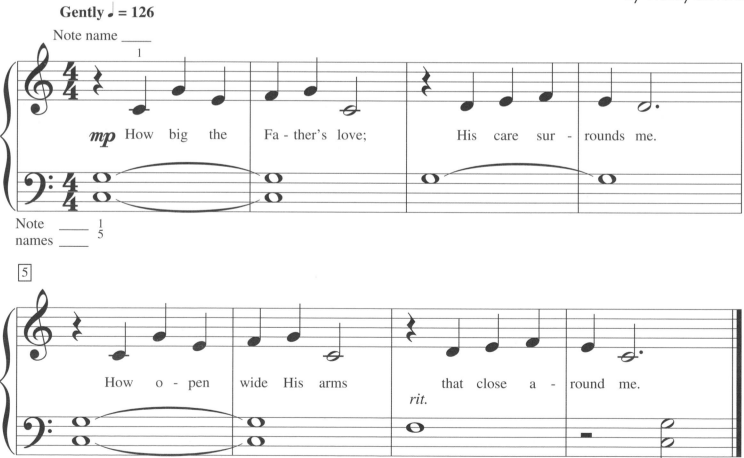

🔊 **TRACKS 53-54**

How Big the Father's Love

By Wendy Stevens

Gently ♩ = 126

Note name ____

mp How big the Fa - ther's love; His care sur - rounds me.

Note ____
names ____

How o - pen wide His arms that close a - round me. *rit.*

Sharps

A sharp sign means to play the next higher note on the keyboard. (This is called a half step.)

A sharp lasts for an entire measure.

F#

F

Draw a sharp sign in this box.

Connect the name of the notes below with the correct note on the keyboard.

C#   A#   F#   G#   D#

TRACKS 55-56

Love the Lord

(Based on Mark 12:30)

By Teresa Ledford

Brightly ♩ = 132

Note name ____

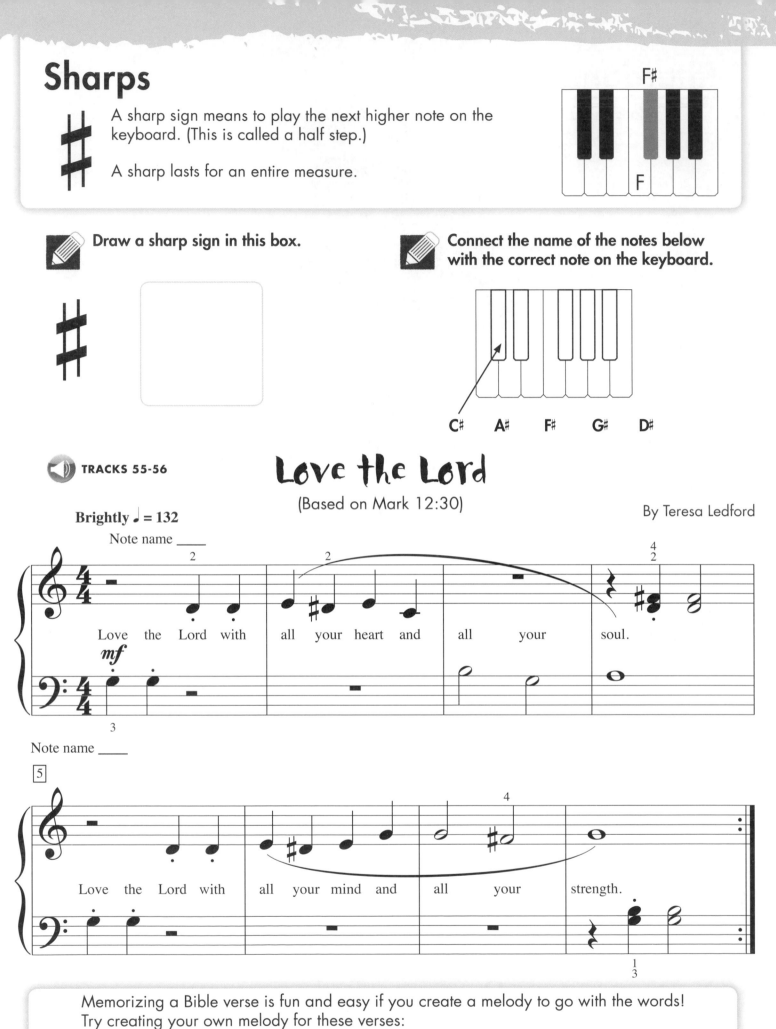

Love the Lord with all your heart and all your soul.

mf

Note name ____

5

Love the Lord with all your mind and all your strength.

Memorizing a Bible verse is fun and easy if you create a melody to go with the words!
Try creating your own melody for these verses:

"Do not fear, for I am with you." – Isaiah 43:5, NASB

"O sing to the Lord a new song, for He has done wonderful things." – Psalm 98:1, NASB

Flats

A flat sign means to play the next lower note on the keyboard. (This is called a half step.)

A flat lasts for an entire measure.

Draw a flat sign in this box.

Connect the name of the notes below with the correct note on the keyboard.

D♭ B♭ G♭ E♭ A♭

TRACKS 57-58

Come, Let Us Sing

By Wendy Stevens

With energy ♩ = 176

This E is also flatted.

Note name ____

Come, let us sing, ___ let us shout, ___ let us wor - ship.

mf

Note name ____

5

We give our praise ___ and our lives ___ to the Lord.

Naturals

A natural sign cancels a sharp or flat.

✎ **Draw a natural sign in this box.**

> "The Lord shows His true love every day. At night I have a song, and I pray to my living God."
>
> – Psalm 42:8, NCV

🔊 **TRACKS 59-60**

I Will Praise You

Moderately fast ♩ = 126

by Teresa Ledford

Note name ____

When   I   pray   qui - et - ly   at   night,   I   will   praise   You.

p

Note ____ names ____

When   I   wake   up   to   morn - ing's   light,   I   will   praise   You.

f

rit.

Matching Accidentals

An **accidental** is a sharp, flat, or natural.

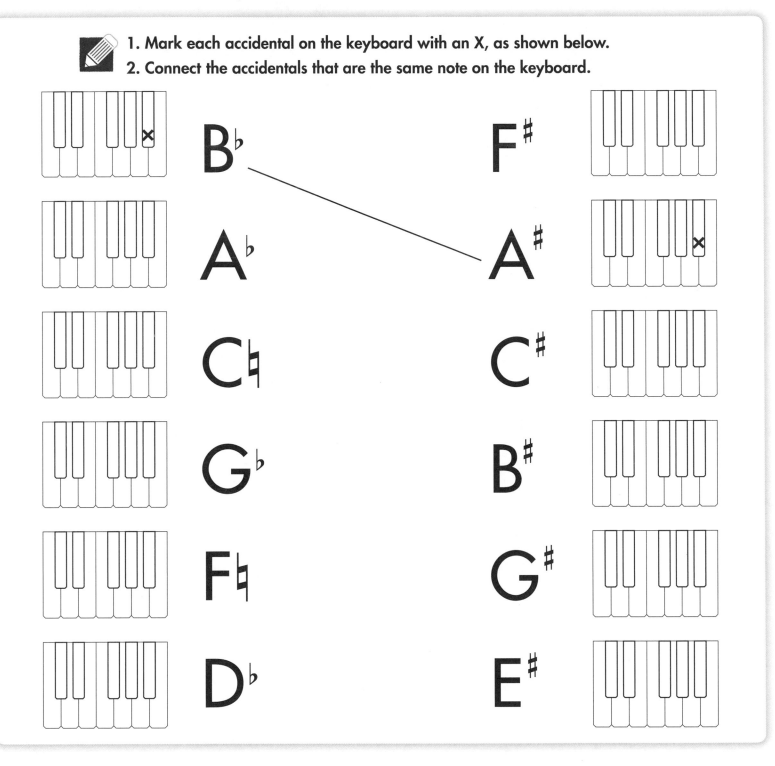

1. Mark each accidental on the keyboard with an X, as shown below.
2. Connect the accidentals that are the same note on the keyboard.

Draw the following accidentals on the same line or space of the note.

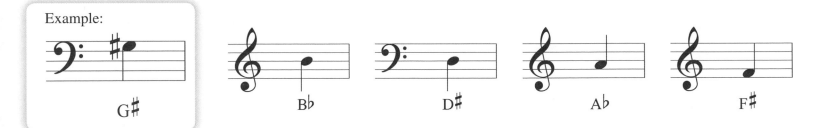

Example:

G♯   B♭   D♯   A♭   F♯

New Notes: High C–G

C   D   E   F   G

call to Worship
(Based on Psalm 95:6)

By Wendy Stevens

With energy ♩ = 168

Note name ____

Come, let   us   wor - ship.   Come, let   us   bow   down.

mf

Note
names ____

Come, let   us   kneel   be - fore the Lord our   Mak - er.

Play this song again, replacing each E with an E♭ (don't use the CD).

Which version do you like best? _____

Right Here

By Teresa Ledford

You're the Worship Leader!

 Gather a group of people around the piano and ask them to sing the "Echo" part after you. Everyone sings "hear me when I pray" and the Chorus together.

 **TRACKS 65-66**

Alpha and Omega

 Which R.H. note never changes throughout the piece? _____

By Wendy Stevens

Accompaniment (Student plays one octave higher than written.)

Confidently ♩ = 126

2nd time rit.

> "'I am the Alpha* and the Omega*,' says the Lord God,
> 'who is and who was and who is to come, the Almighty.'"
> – Revelation 1:8, NASB

*These Greek words mean "beginning" and "end." *Omega* is pronounced "oh-MAY-guh."

I Am Bound for the Promised Land

Longingly ♩ = 144

Traditional
Arranged by Wendy Stevens

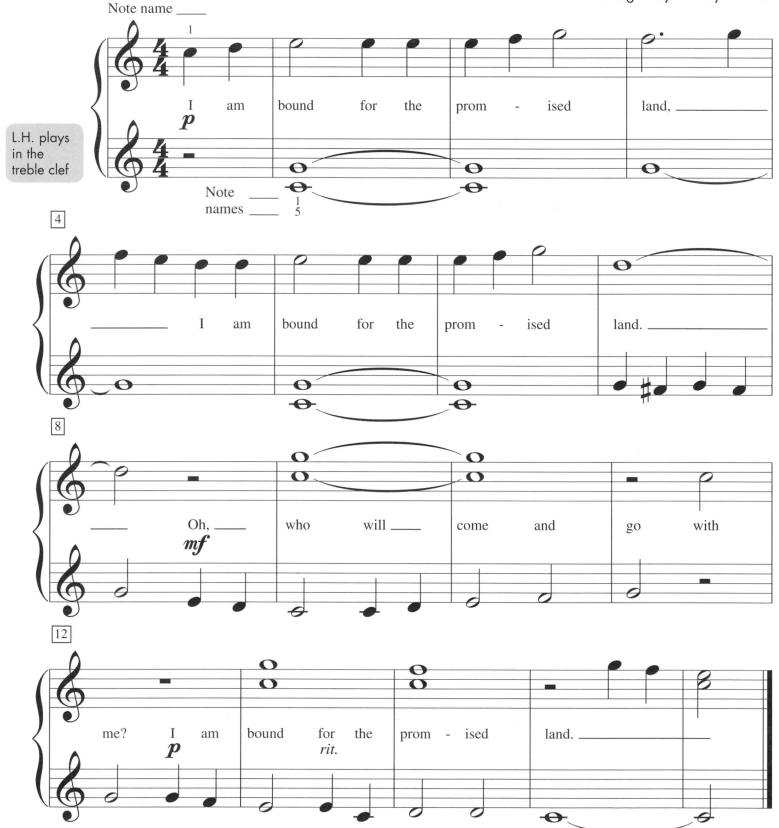

L.H. plays in the treble clef

1st & 2nd Endings

1st time:
Play only the first
ending before
you repeat.

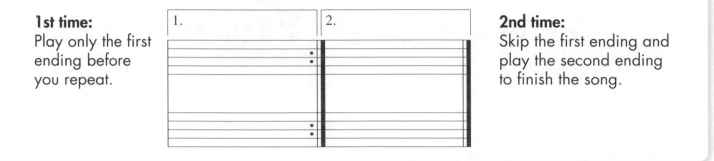

2nd time:
Skip the first ending and
play the second ending
to finish the song.

"...The words I have spoken to you are spirit and are life."
– John 6:63, NASB

TRACKS 69-70 Wonderful Words of Life

Sweetly ♩ = 189

Words and Music by Philip P. Bliss
Arranged by Wendy Stevens

L.H. plays
in the
treble clef

Note name ____

Sing   them   o - ver a - gain   to   me,

mf

Note ____
names ____

won - der - ful   words   of   life. ____   Let   me

more   of   their   beau - ty   see,   won - der - ful   words   of

56

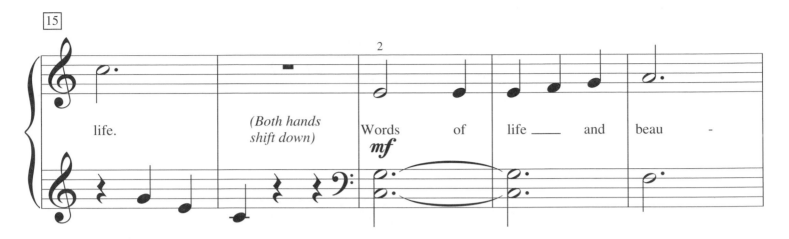

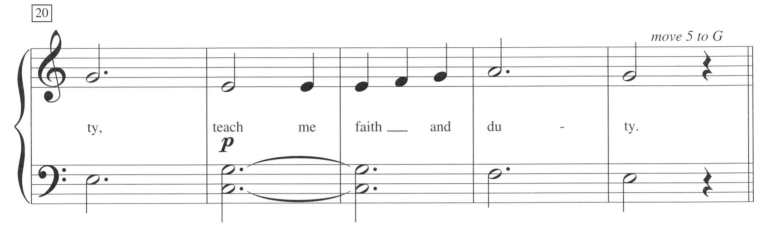

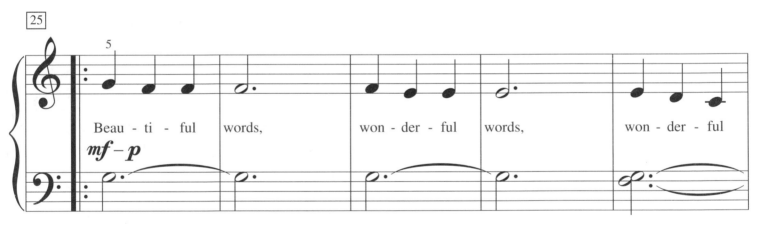

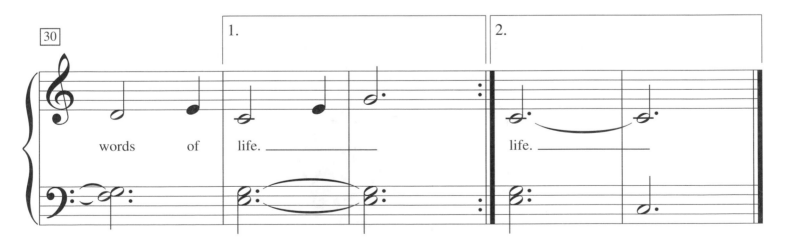

New Notes: Low G, A, B

G A B C D

new notes

TRACKS 71-72

Lord, I Will Sing

By Teresa Ledford

Brightly ♩ = 138

Note name ____

3

mf Lord, I will sing for You all my days. ____

Note name ____

5

5

I lift my hands and my heart in praise. ____

"I will praise You as long as I live. I will lift up my hands in prayer to Your name."

– Psalm 63:4, NCV

58

TRACKS 73-74

My Hands Are His

Quickly ♩ = 180

By Wendy Stevens

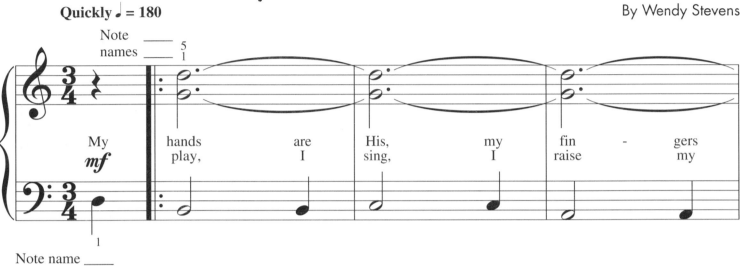

Note names _____ 5
_____ 1

My
mf

My hands are His, my fin - gers my
play, I sing, raise

Note name ____
1

too; my lips, my voice, and
hands to give Him praise as

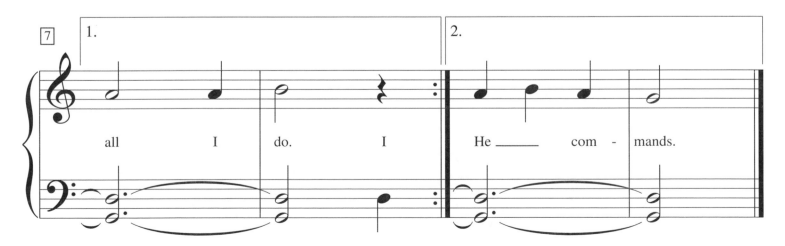

1.
all I do. I

2.
He ____ com - mands.

> "Whatever you do in word or deed, do all in the name of the Lord Jesus, giving thanks through Him to God the Father."
> – Colossians 3:17, NASB

My Song of Praise (G A B C D)

Compose your own praise song using only G A B C D.
Draw your notes on the staff using the rhythm given.

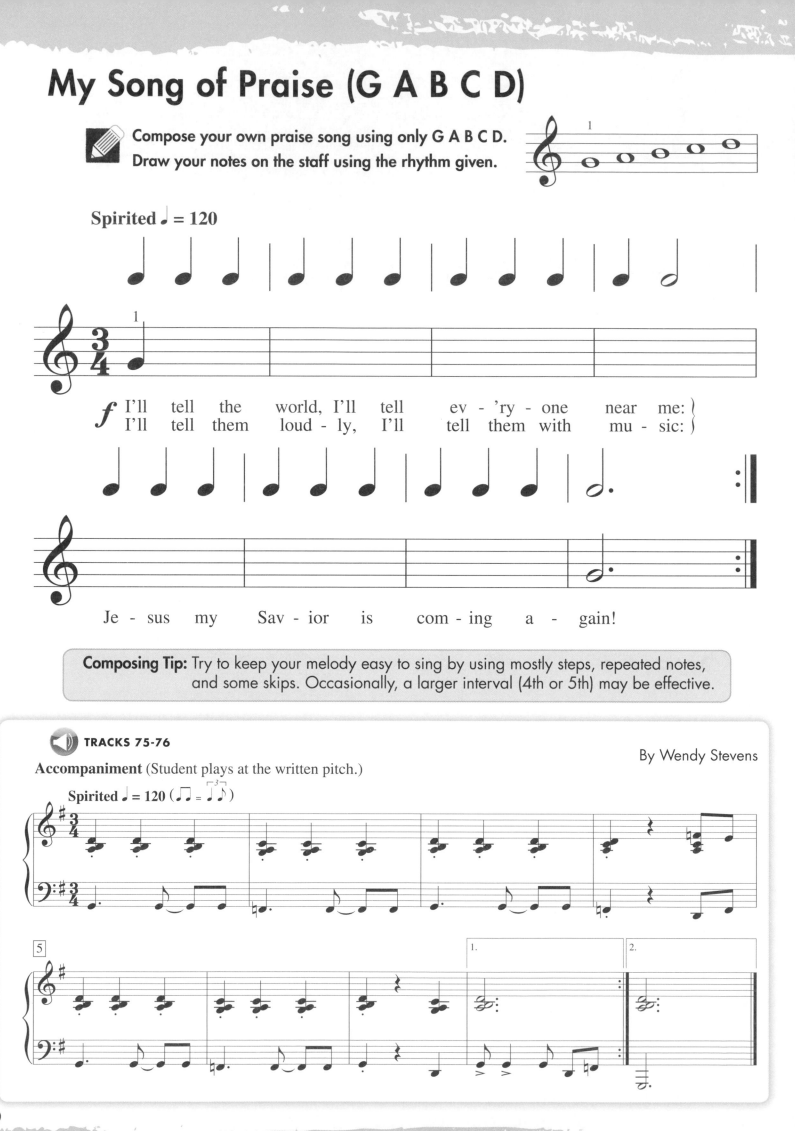

Spirited ♩ = 120

𝆑 I'll tell the world, I'll tell ev-'ry-one near me:
I'll tell them loud-ly, I'll tell them with mu-sic:

Je - sus my Sav - ior is com - ing a - gain!

Composing Tip: Try to keep your melody easy to sing by using mostly steps, repeated notes, and some skips. Occasionally, a larger interval (4th or 5th) may be effective.

🔊 **TRACKS 75-76**

By Wendy Stevens

Accompaniment (Student plays at the written pitch.)

Spirited ♩ = 120 (♫ = ♪)

Crescendo & Diminuendo

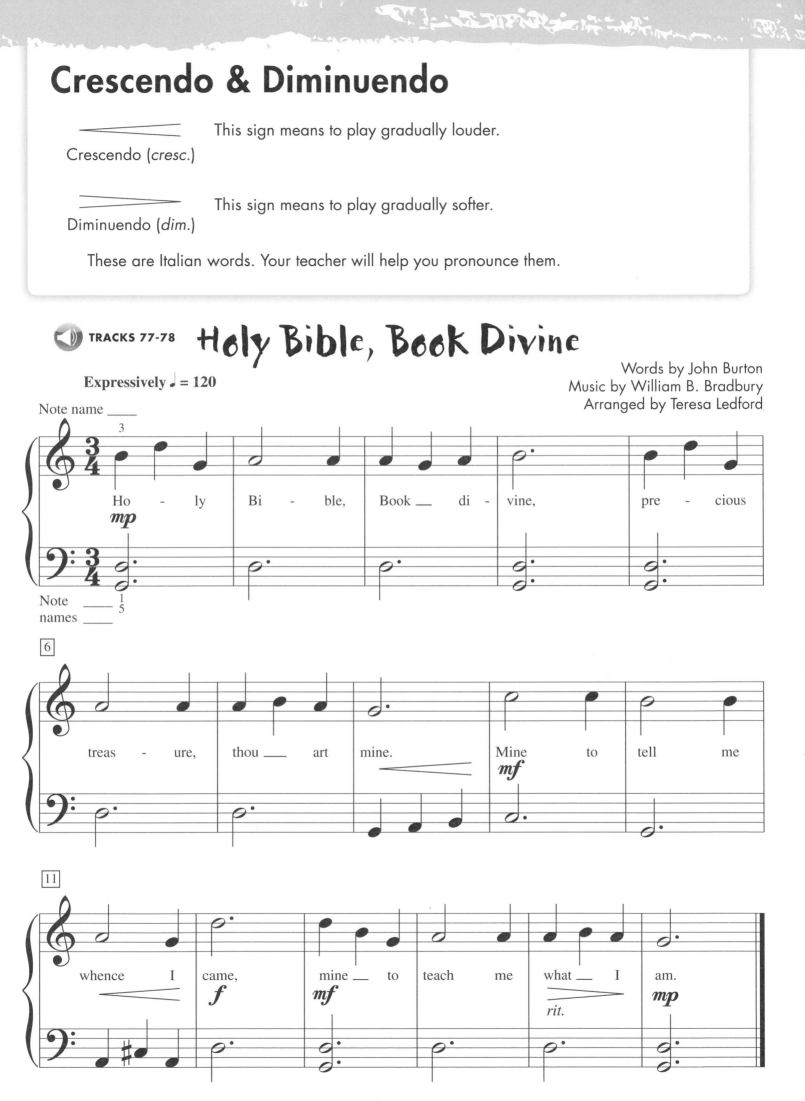

Crescendo (*cresc.*)

This sign means to play gradually louder.

Diminuendo (*dim.*)

This sign means to play gradually softer.

These are Italian words. Your teacher will help you pronounce them.

TRACKS 77-78

Holy Bible, Book Divine

Words by John Burton
Music by William B. Bradbury
Arranged by Teresa Ledford

Expressively ♩ = 120

Note name ____

Ho - ly Bi - ble, Book __ di - vine, pre - cious

mp

Note names ____

treas - ure, thou __ art mine. Mine to tell me

mf

whence I came, mine __ to teach me what __ I am.

f *mf* *rit.* *mp*

D.S. al Fine

 D.S. al Fine means to go back to the measure marked with the  sign and end at the measure marked **Fine**.

TRACKS 79-80

Give Him Glory

Brightly ♩ = 192

Words by Teresa Ledford
Music by Wendy Stevens

Note name _____

Give Him glo-ry, make a joy-ful noise.

Note name _____

Give Him glo-ry, lift-ing up _____ your voice.

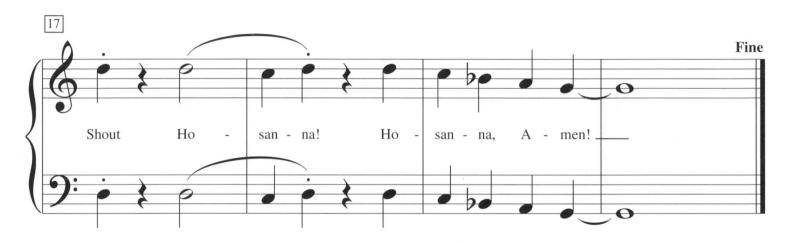

13 Give Him glo - ry, let the praise _____ be - gin.

17 Shout Ho - san - na! Ho - san - na, A - men! _____ **Fine**

21 He is ho - ly, and we will pro - claim: _____ *mf*

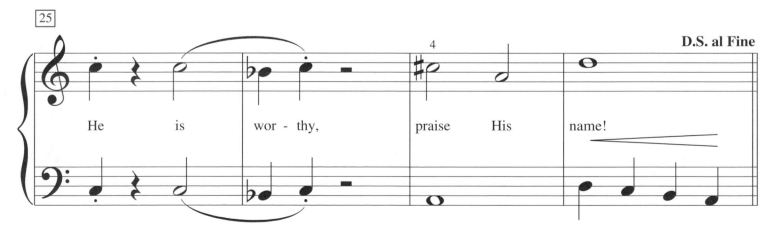

25 He is wor - thy, praise His name! **D.S. al Fine**

CONGRATULATIONS!

_____
(Student Name)

has completed Level 1 of

the
WorshiP
PIANO METHOD

and is hereby promoted to Level 2.

Celebrate this achievement by playing your
favorite pieces for your family and friends!

Date _____   Teacher _____